SADLER'S WELLS BALLET AT COVENT GARDEN

also by Merlyn Severn BALLET IN ACTION *with an introduction by* Arnold L. Haskell

SADLER'S WELLS BALLET AT COVENT GARDEN

A BOOK OF PHOTOGRAPHS BY MERLYN SEVERN

JOHN LANE THE BODLEY HEAD : LONDON 1947

First published in 1947 by John Lane The Bodley Head Ltd., 8 Bury Place, London, W.C.1
and printed in Great Britain by The Vandyck Printers Ltd., London and Bristol.

ACKNOWLEDGEMENTS

A GOOD many of the photographs of 'The Sleeping Beauty' were originally taken for *Picture Post*, and are reproduced here by courtesy of the editor.   I should also like to express my thanks to Frederick Ashton and Joy Newton for valuable help in preparing the book.

All the pictures were taken with a Contax II camera, most of them with the 8.5 cm. lens. The photographs of 'Symphonic Variations' were taken through a green filter—a tribute to the speed of the Selo H.P.3 film on which they, as well as all the other pictures, were taken.

PHOTOGRAPHS

(The dancers are named from left to right)

frontispiece Palma Nye, Robert Helpmann, Jean Bedells (*Adam Zero*)

The Sleeping Beauty

1 Anne Negus, Nadia Narina, Margaret Dady, David Davenport, Julia Farron.
2 Pauline Clayden.
3 Gerd Larsen, Margaret Dale.
4 Beryl Grey.
5 Gillian Lynne.
6 Anne Negus.
7 Julia Farron, David Davenport, Leslie Edwards.
8 Robert Helpmann, Julia Farron.
9 Gerd Larsen, Robert Helpmann, Margaret Dale, Joan Sheldon.
10 Bridget Gladwell, Ann Horne, Pamela Harford, Geraldine Grundy, Leslie Edwards.
11 Corps de Ballet.
12 Margot Fonteyn.
13 Avril Navarre, Margaret Roseby, Oenone Talbot, Joan Sheldon, Margot Fonteyn.
14 Margot Fonteyn.
15 Margot Fonteyn, Anthony Burke.
16 Margot Fonteyn, Norman Thomson.
17 Norman Thomson, Margot Fonteyn, Julia Farron.
18 Margot Fonteyn.
19 Margot Fonteyn.
20 Leslie Edwards, Margot Fonteyn, David Davenport, Robert Helpmann, Anne Negus.

21   Leslie Edwards, Margot Fonteyn, Julia Farron, Beryl Grey.

22   Jean Bedells, David Paltenghi.

23   Robert Helpmann.

24   Margot Fonteyn, Beryl Grey, Robert Helpmann, Guinevere Parry.

25   Margot Fonteyn, Robert Helpmann.

26   Anne Negus, Henry Danton, Gerd Larsen.

27   Oenone Talbot, Stanley Holden.

28   Violetta Prokhorova, Alexis Rassine.

29   Violetta Prokhorova, Alexis Rassine.

30   Richard Ellis, June Leighton.

31   Franklin White, Donald Britton, Gordon Hamilton.

32   Margot Fonteyn, Robert Helpmann.

33   Margot Fonteyn, Robert Helpmann.

34   Margot Fonteyn, Robert Helpmann.

35   Grand Finale.

Miracle in the Gorbals

36   Henry Danton, David Paltenghi, Palma Nye, Franklin White, Leslie Edwards.

37   Joy Newton, Palma Nye, Pauline Clayden, Gerd Larsen.

38   Tony Tarver, David Paltenghi, Franklin White, Pauline Clayden.

39   Robert Helpmann.

40   Robert Helpmann, Pauline Clayden.

41   Michael Somes, Pauline Clayden.

42   Michael Somes, David Paltenghi.

43 Pauline Clayden, David Paltenghi, Michael Somes.

44 David Paltenghi, Paul Reymond.

45 Henry Danton, David Davenport, Franklin White, Michael Somes, Anthony Burke, Brian Shaw, Kenneth Melville.

46 Julia Farron, Pauline Clayden, Michael Somes, Leslie Edwards.

47 Leslie Edwards, Robert Helpmann.

The Rake's Progress

48 David Paltenghi, Anthony Burke, Robert Helpmann, Paul Reymond, Leslie Edwards.

49 Robert Helpmann, Gordon Hamilton.

50 Elizabeth Kennedy, Margot Fonteyn, Robert Helpmann, Gordon Hamilton.

51 Elizabeth Kennedy, Gordon Hamilton, Robert Helpmann, Margot Fonteyn.

52 Joy Newton, Leslie Edwards, Joan Sheldon, Jill Gregory, Palma Nye, June Leighton, Gerd Larsen, Robert Helpmann.

53 Joan Sheldon, Joy Newton, Palma Nye, Jill Gregory, Harold Turner, Moira Shearer.

54 Leslie Edwards, Margot Fonteyn, Anthony Burke, Franklin White, Robert Helpmann.

55 Franklin White, Leslie Edwards, Anthony Burke, Julia Farron, Harold Turner.

56 Robert Helpmann.

57 Julia Farron, Robert Helpmann.

Symphonic Variations

58 Margot Fonteyn, Pamela May, Henry Danton, Brian Shaw, Moira Shearer.

59 Moira Shearer, Michael Somes, Margot Fonteyn, Pamela May.

60 Henry Danton, Moira Shearer, Michael Somes, Margot Fonteyn.

61 Henry Danton, Moira Shearer, Michael Somes, Margot Fonteyn.

PHOTOGRAPHS

Adam Zero

62 Robert Helpmann, corps de ballet.

63 Palma Nye, Robert Helpmann, Jean Bedells.

64 June Brae, Robert Helpmann.

65 Robert Helpmann, Leslie Edwards, June Brae.

66 Jill Gregory, Guinevere Parry, Paula Dunning, Leslie Edwards, Robert Helpmann, June Brae, Rosemary Lindsay.

67 Denis Carey, Gordon Hamilton, Robert Helpmann, Gillian Lynne, Alexis Rassine, David Paltenghi, Palma Nye, Veronica Vail.

68 Robert Helpmann, June Brae.

69 Julia Farron, Palma Nye, June Brae, Robert Helpmann, Alexis Rassine, David Paltenghi.

70 Julia Farron, Alexis Rassine, Robert Helpmann, David Paltenghi.

71 Leslie Edwards, David Paltenghi, Robert Helpmann, Jean Bedells, Palma Nye, Julia Farron.

72 David Paltenghi, Robert Helpmann.

73 Robert Helpmann, Joan Sheldon, Kenneth Melville, Norman Thomson.

74 June Brae, Robert Helpmann.

75 Palma Nye, Julia Farron, Jean Bedells, Robert Helpmann.

76 Robert Helpmann, David Paltenghi, Leslie Edwards.

77 Leslie Edwards, Robert Helpmann.

78 June Brae, Robert Helpmann.

79 June Brae, Robert Helpmann.

80 June Brae, Robert Helpmann.

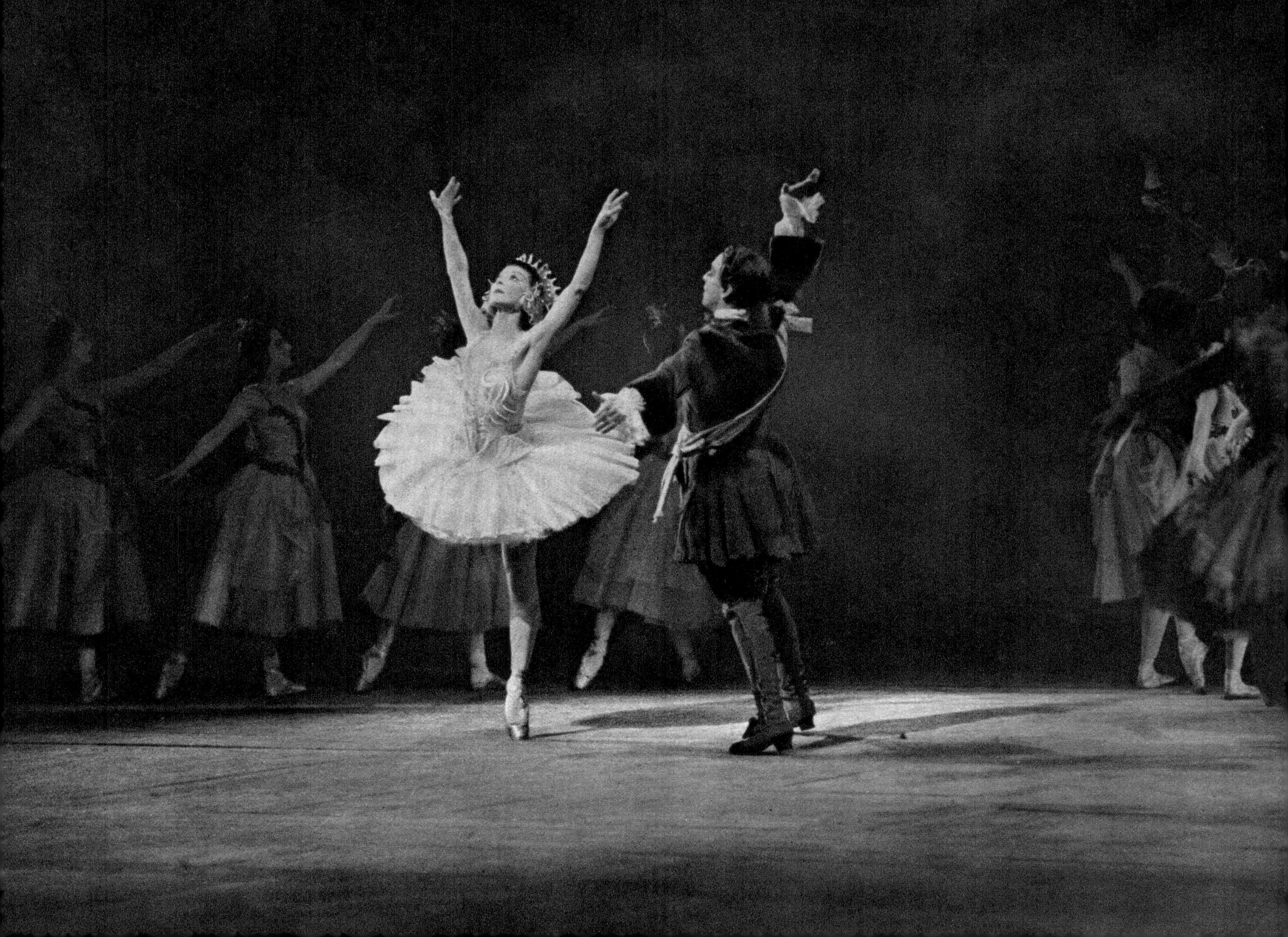

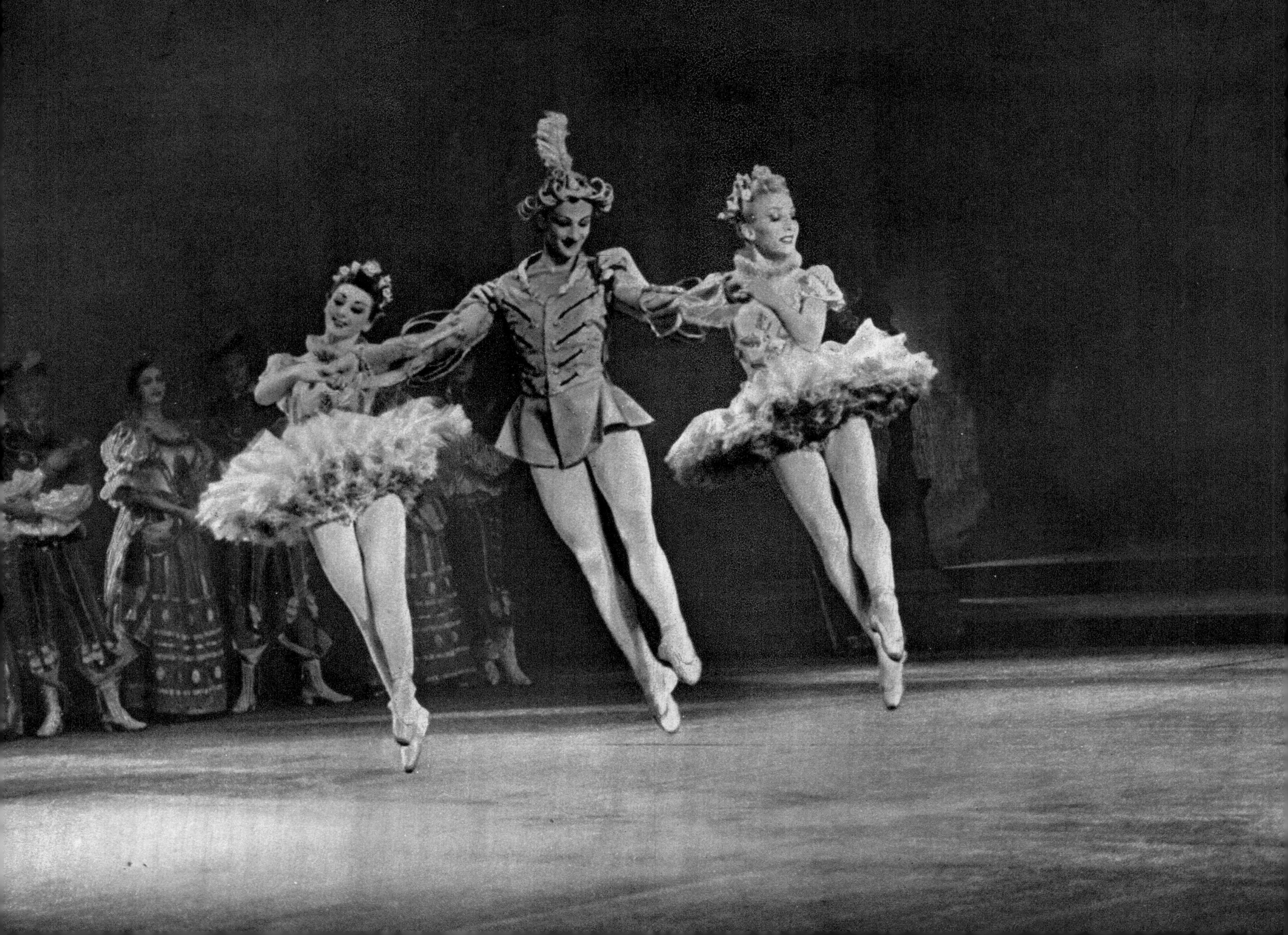

38 MIRACLE IN THE GORBALS Helpmann

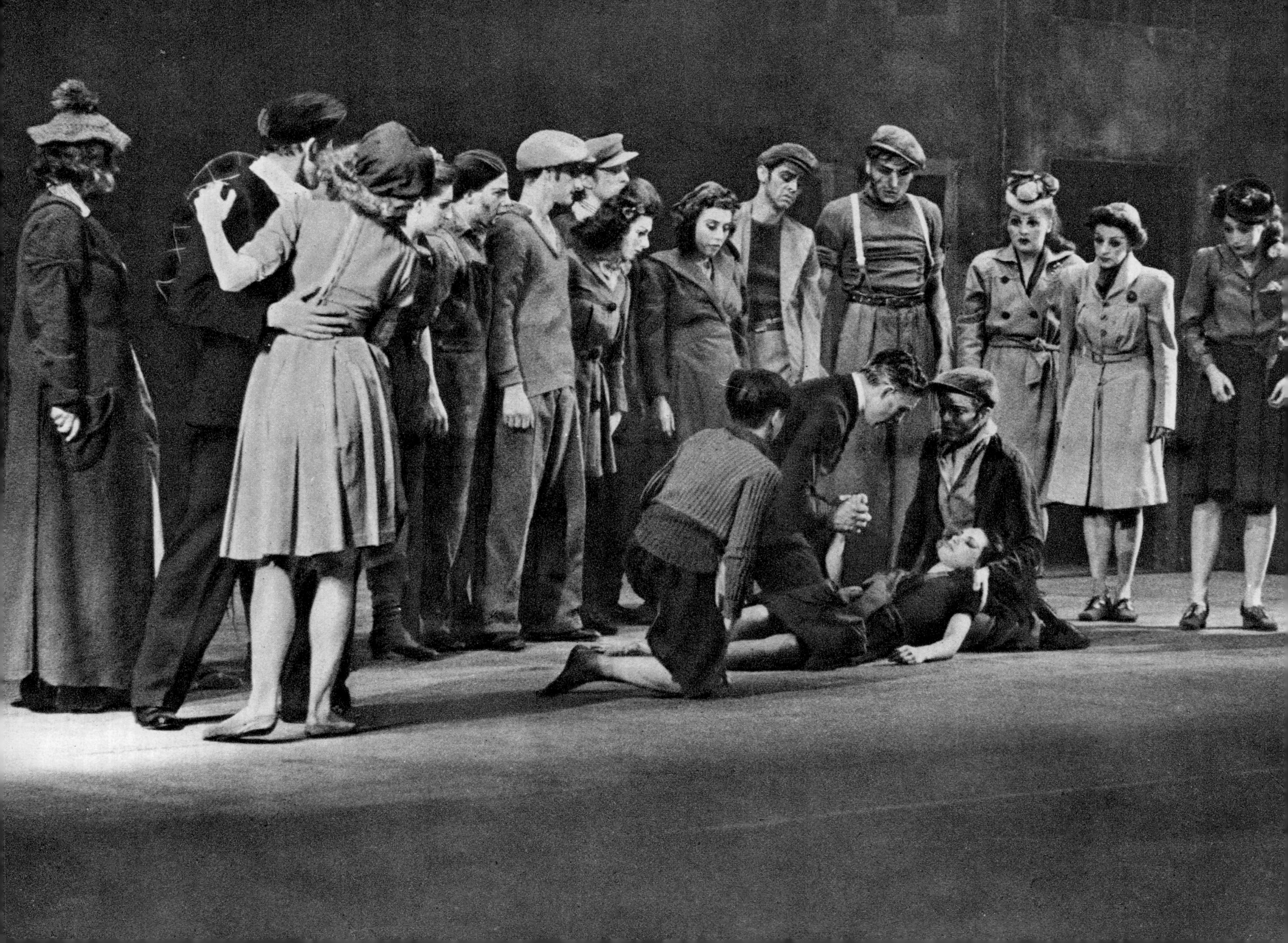

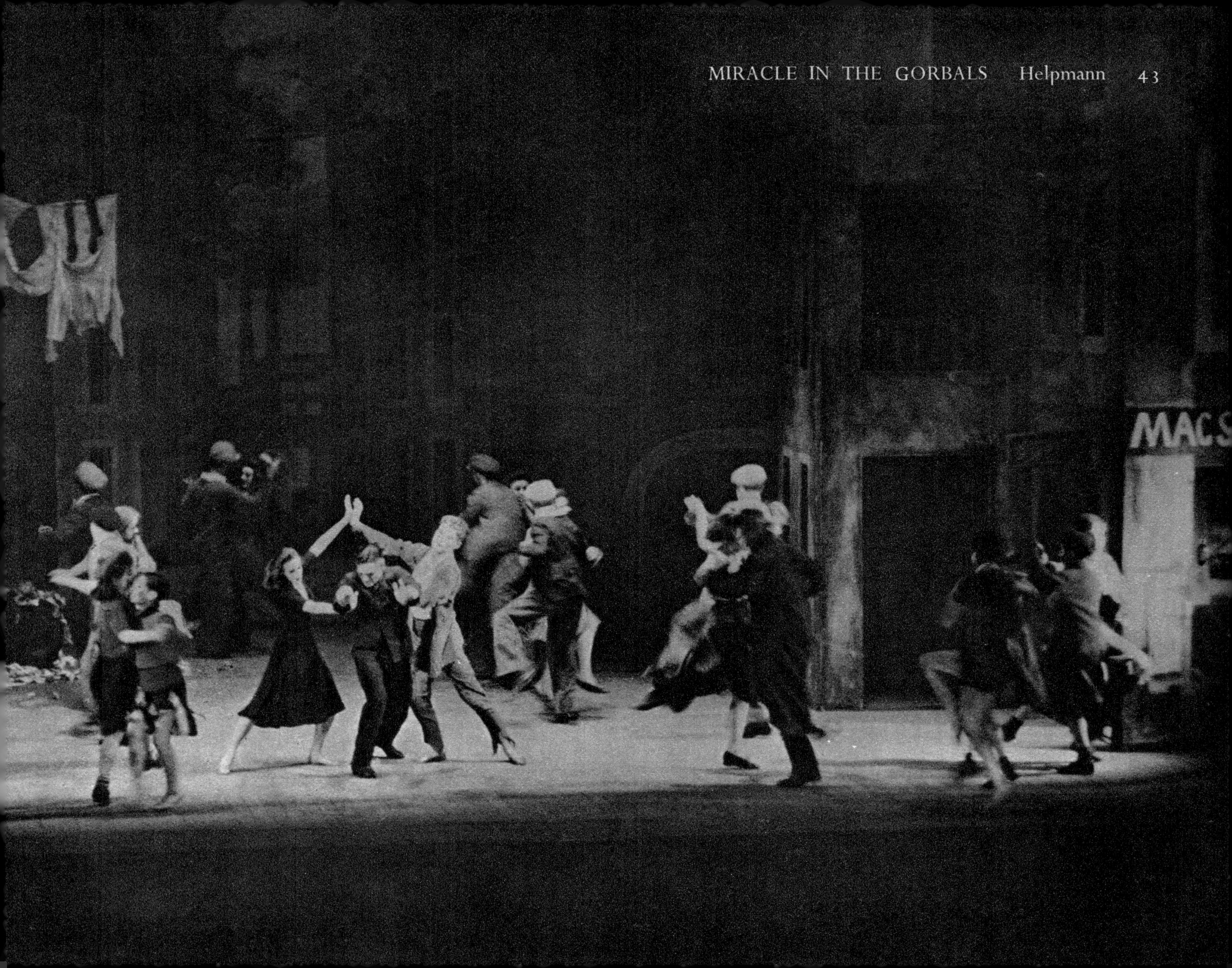
MACS

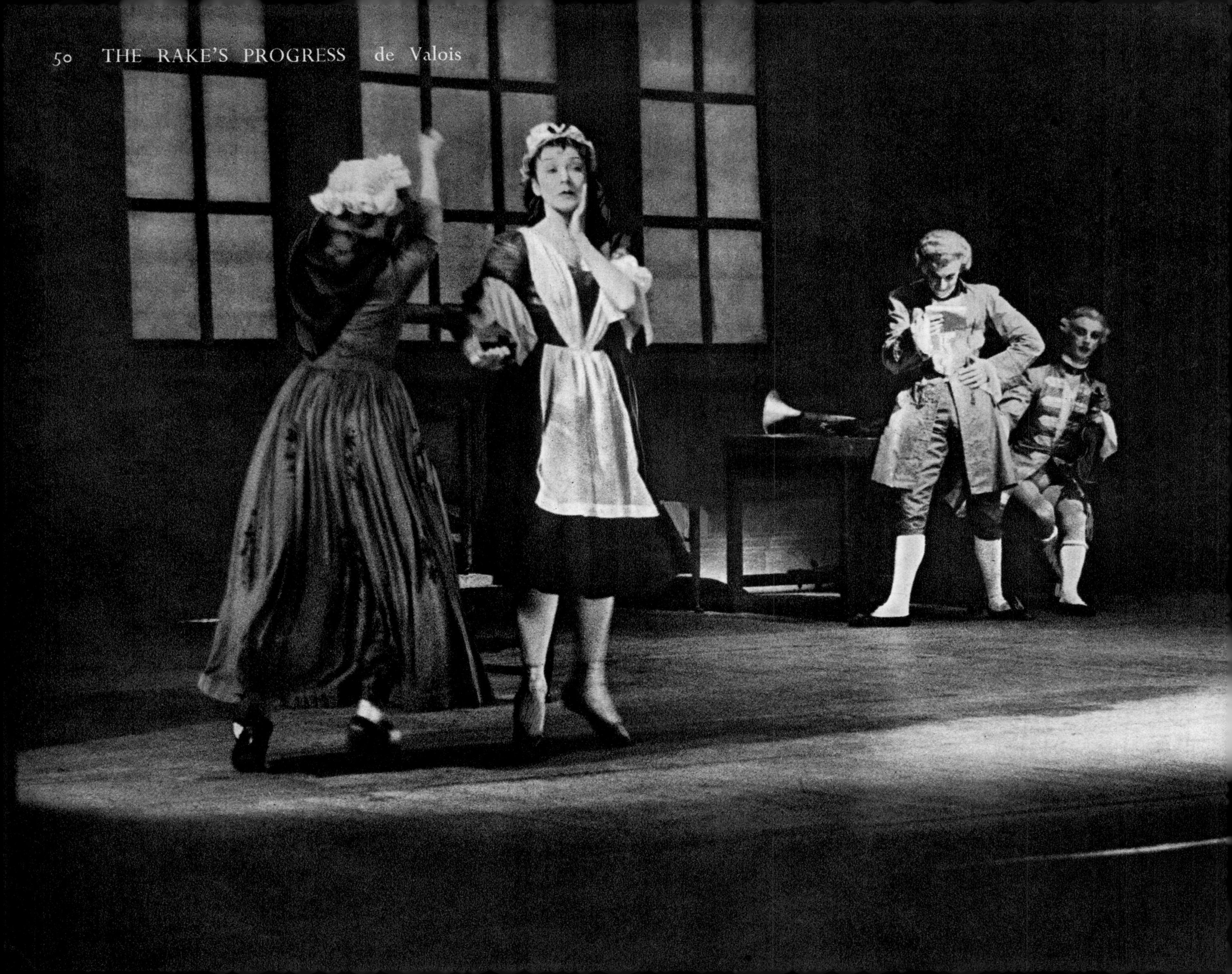

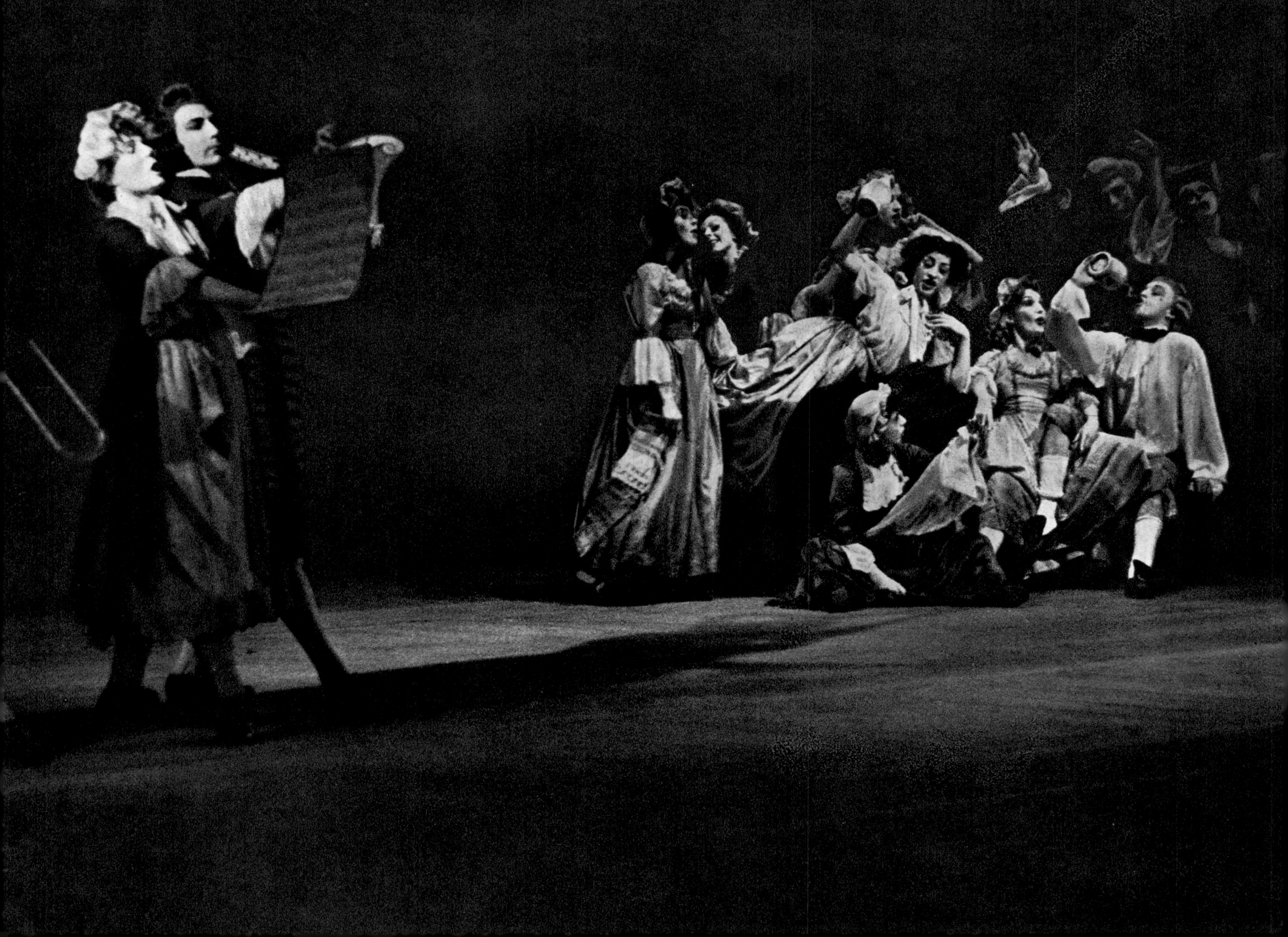

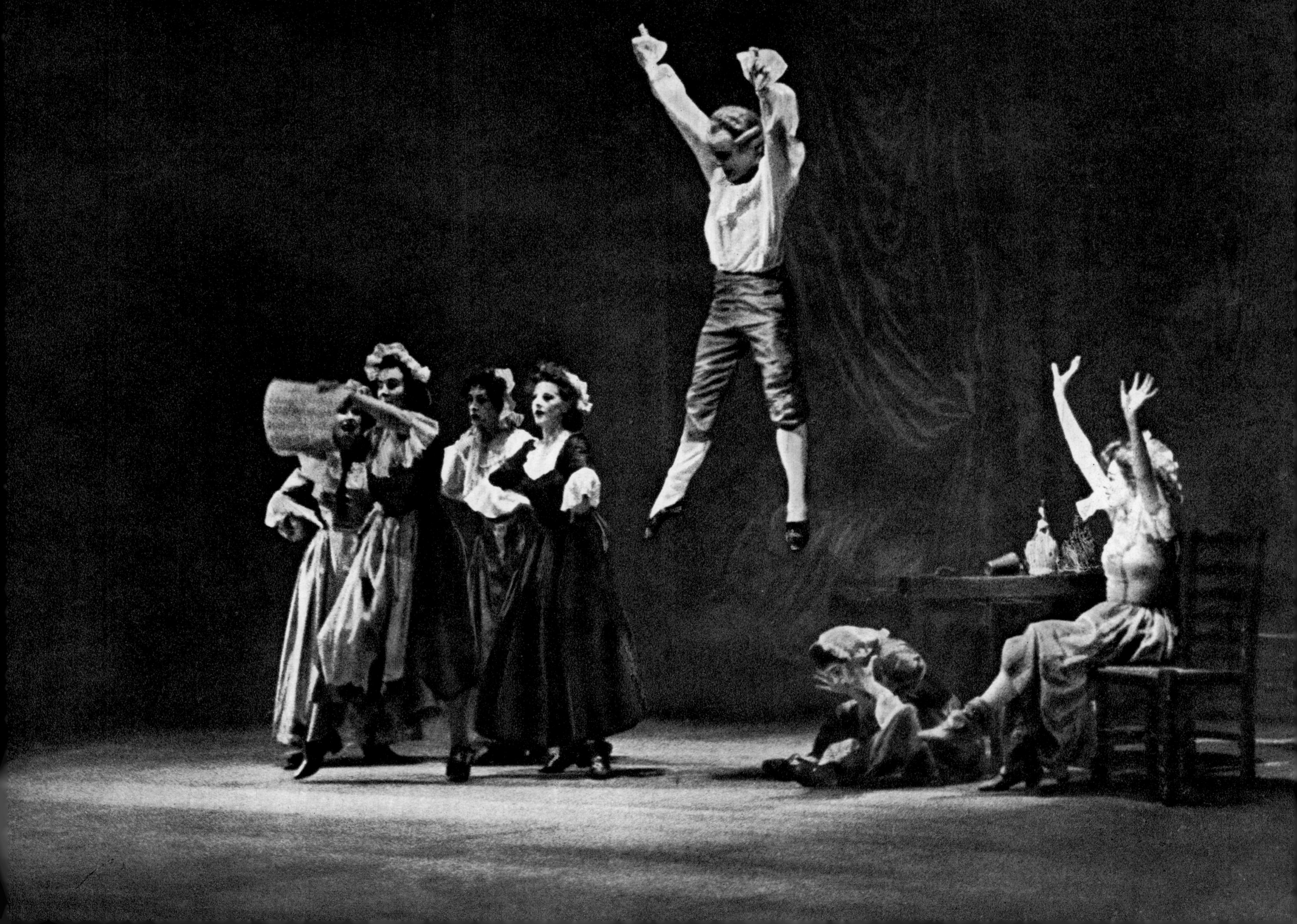

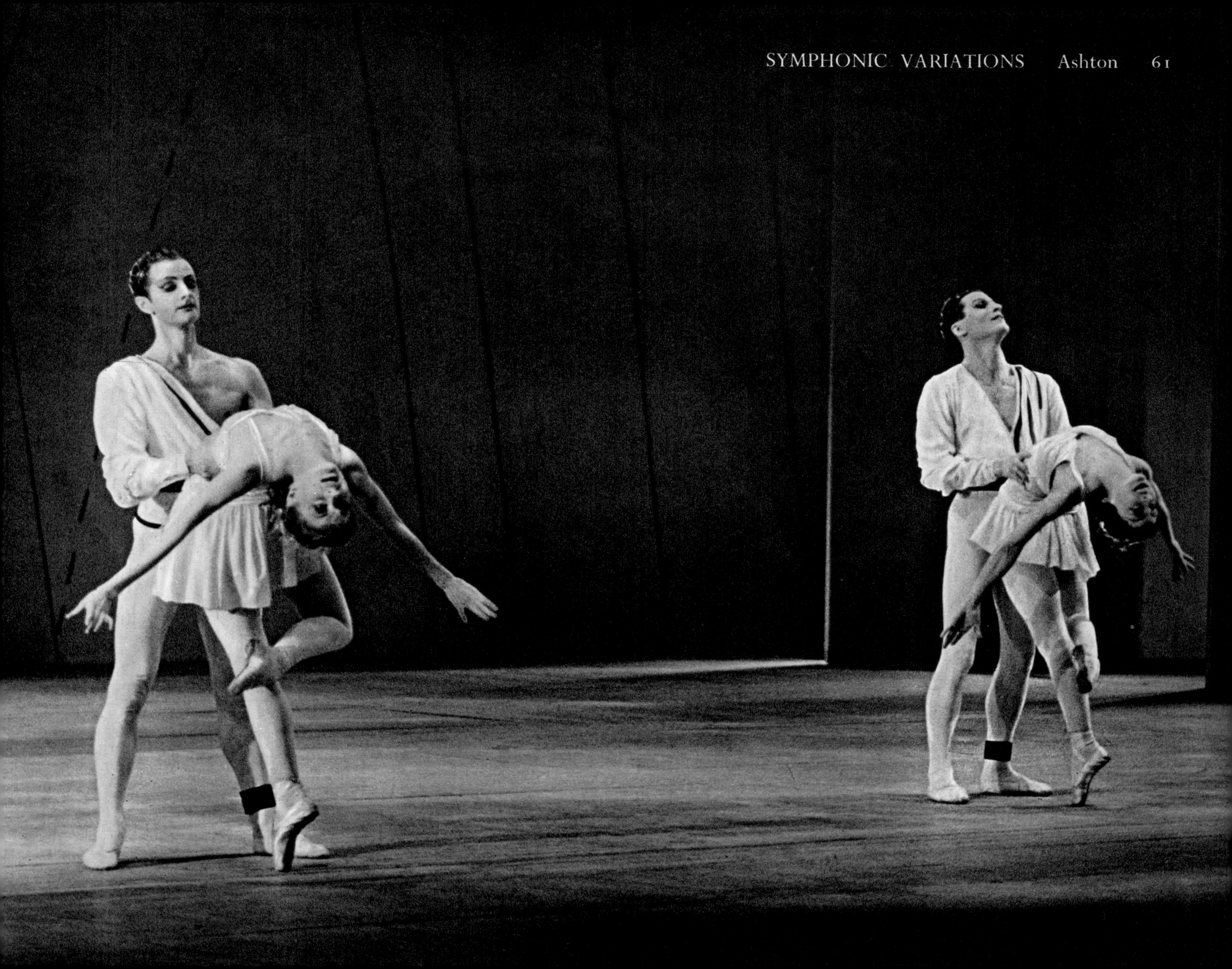

62 ADAM ZERO Helpmann

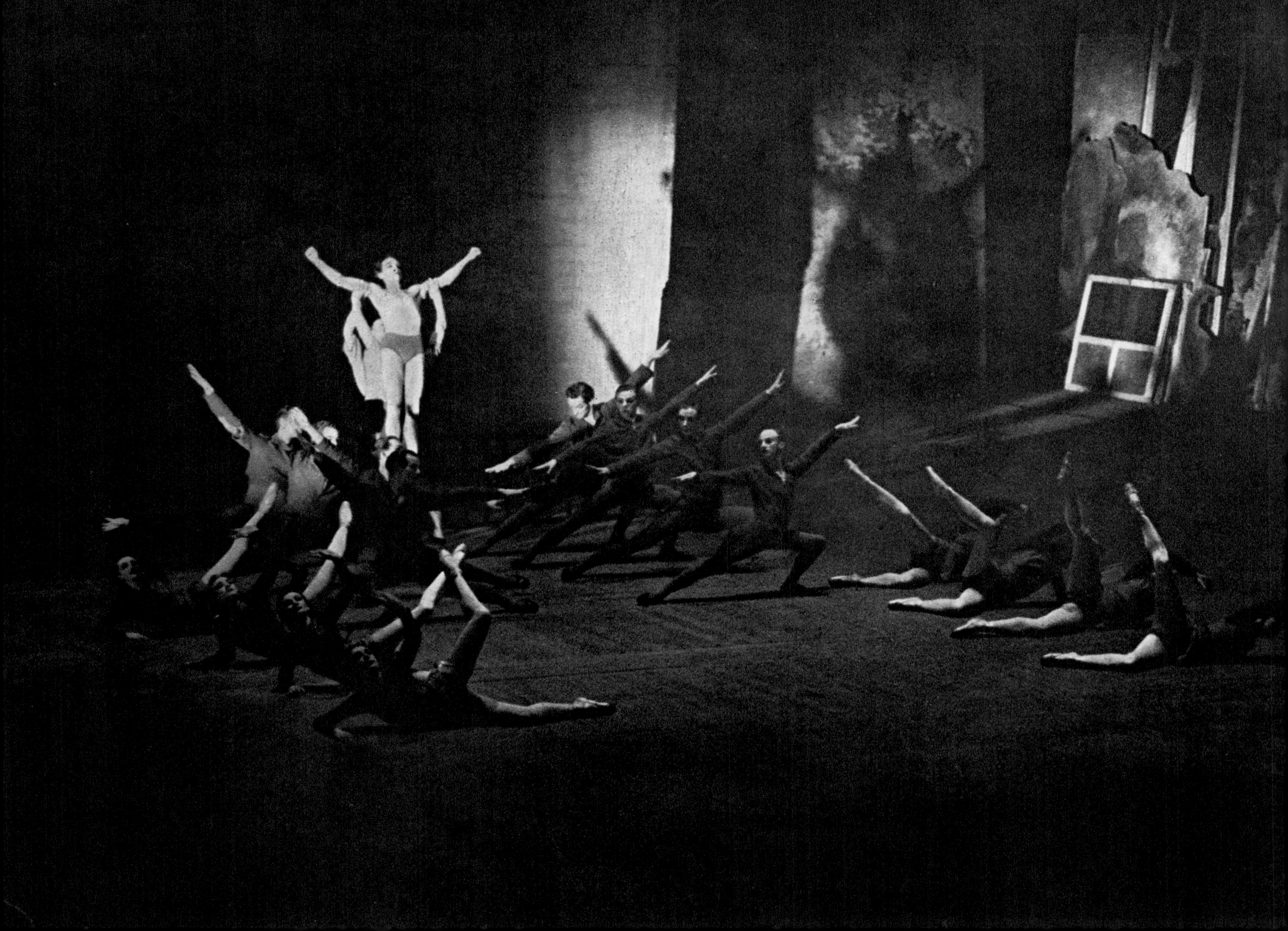

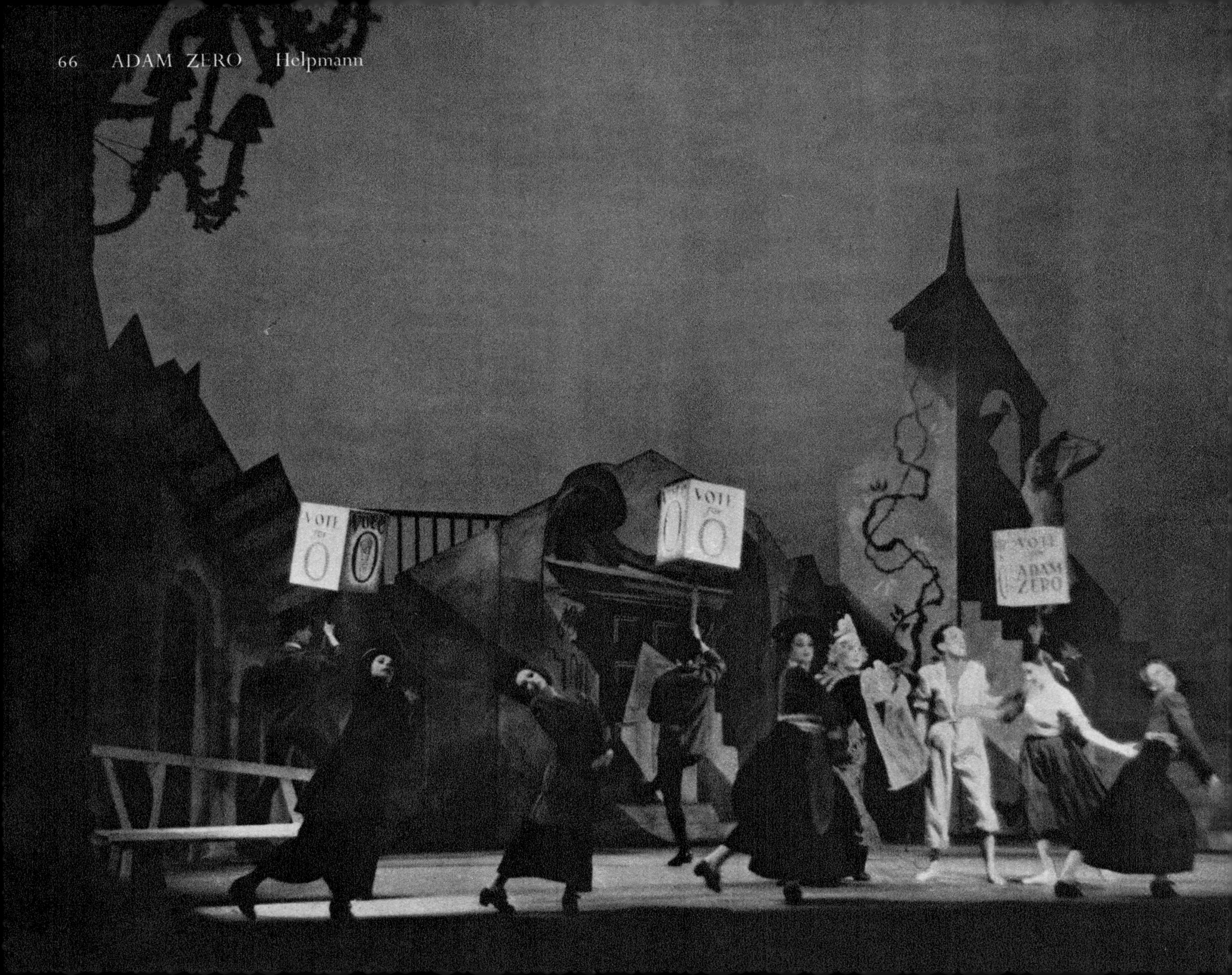
VOTE for O
VOTE for O
VOTE for ADAM ZERO

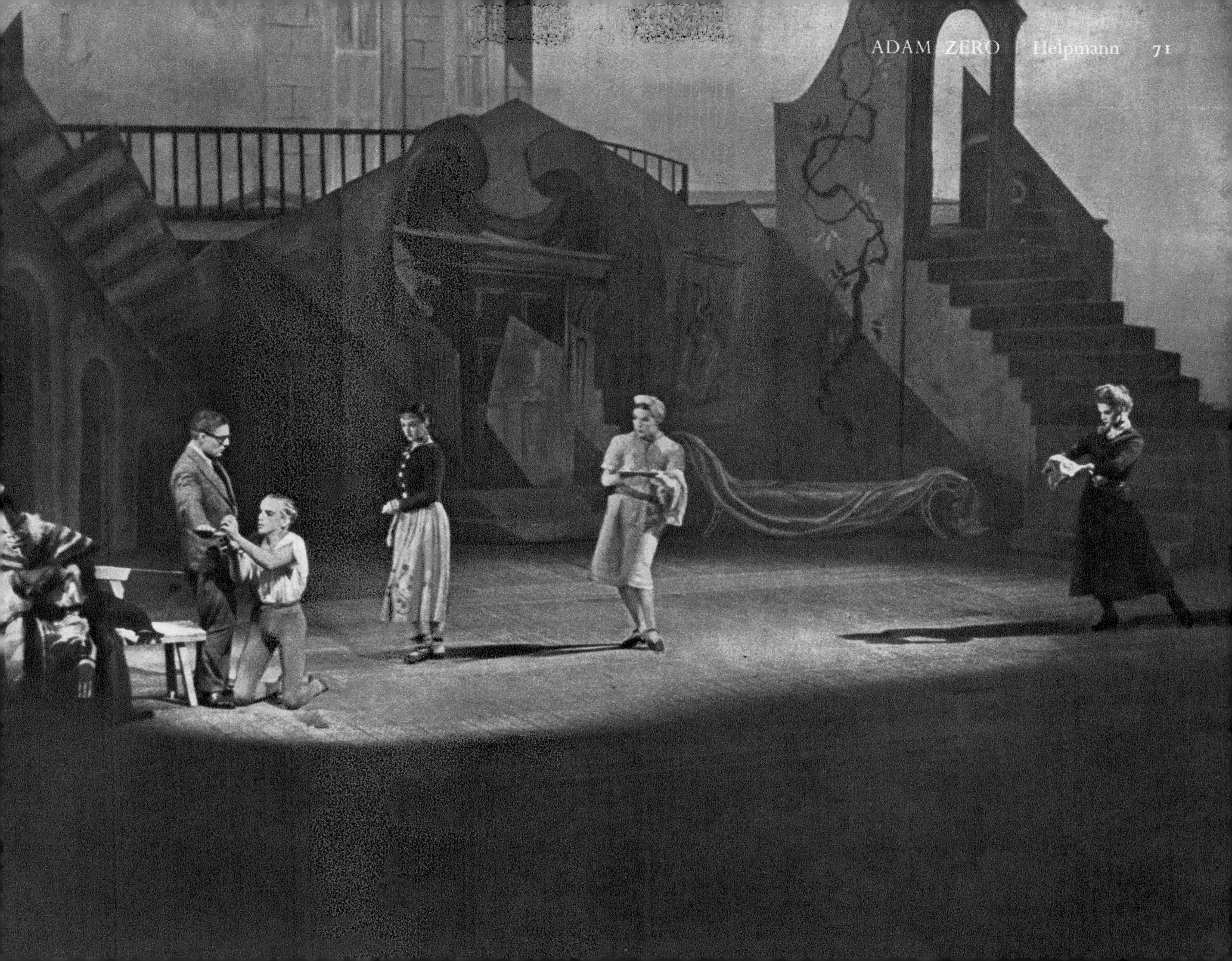

74 ADAM ZERO Helpmann

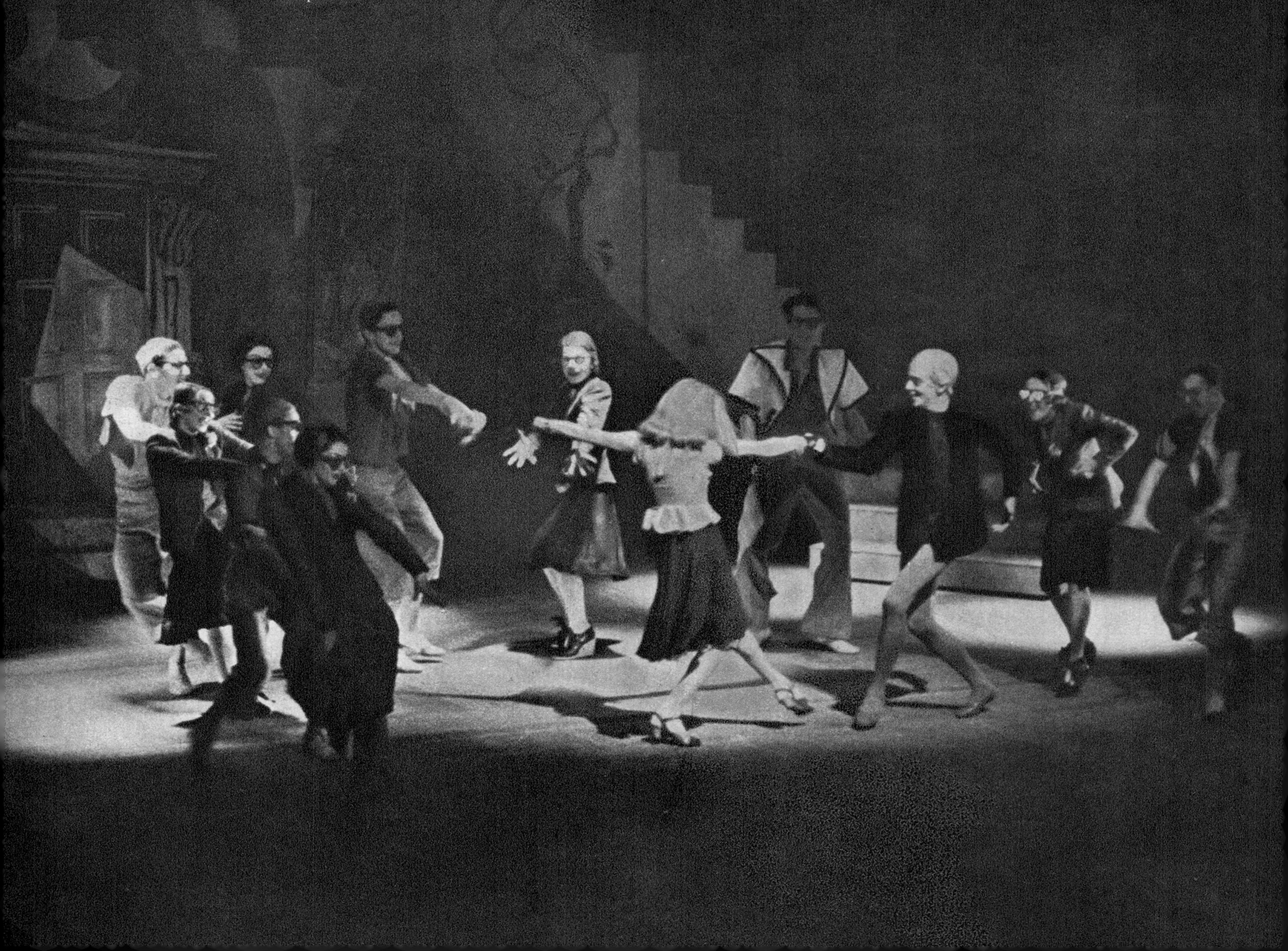

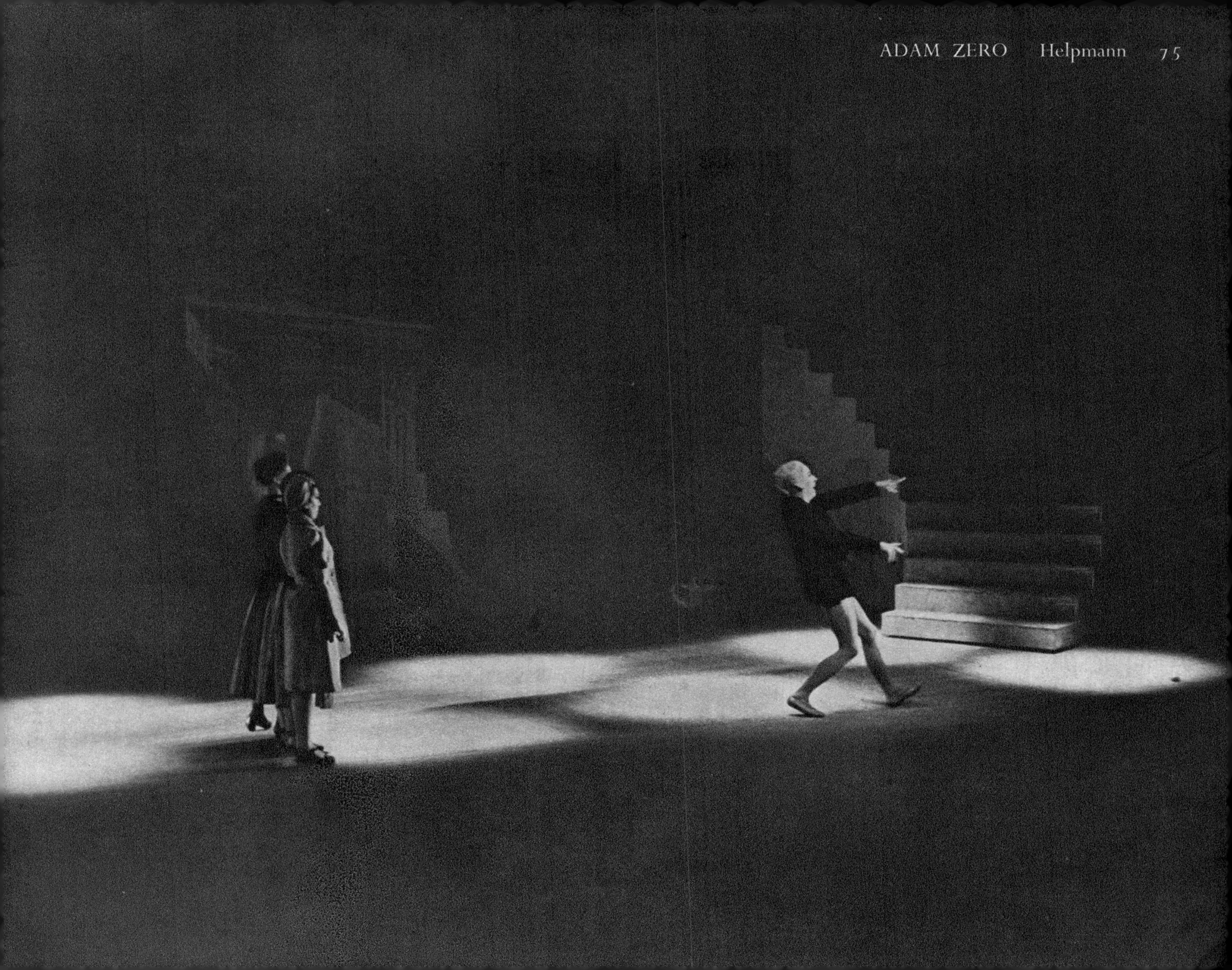

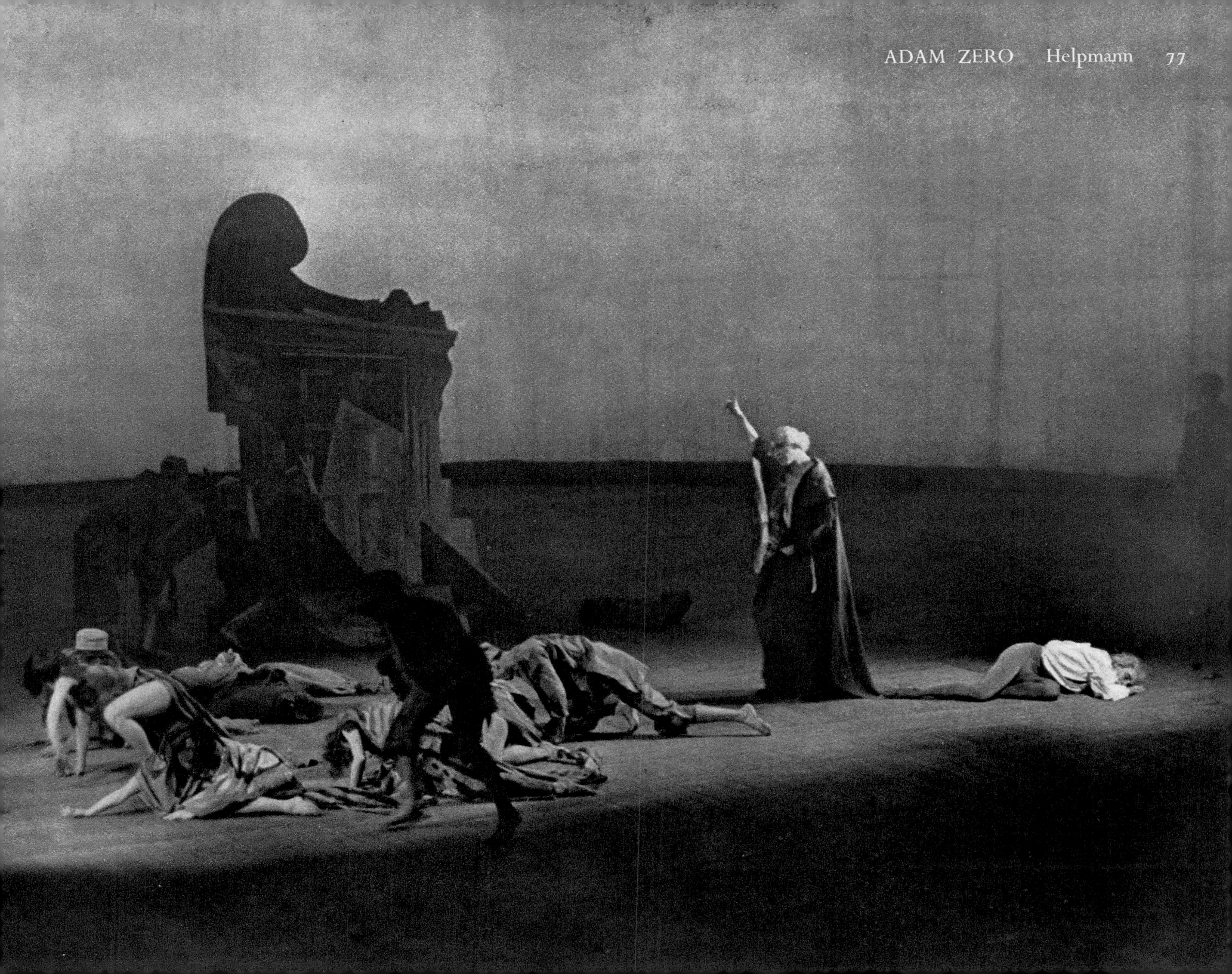

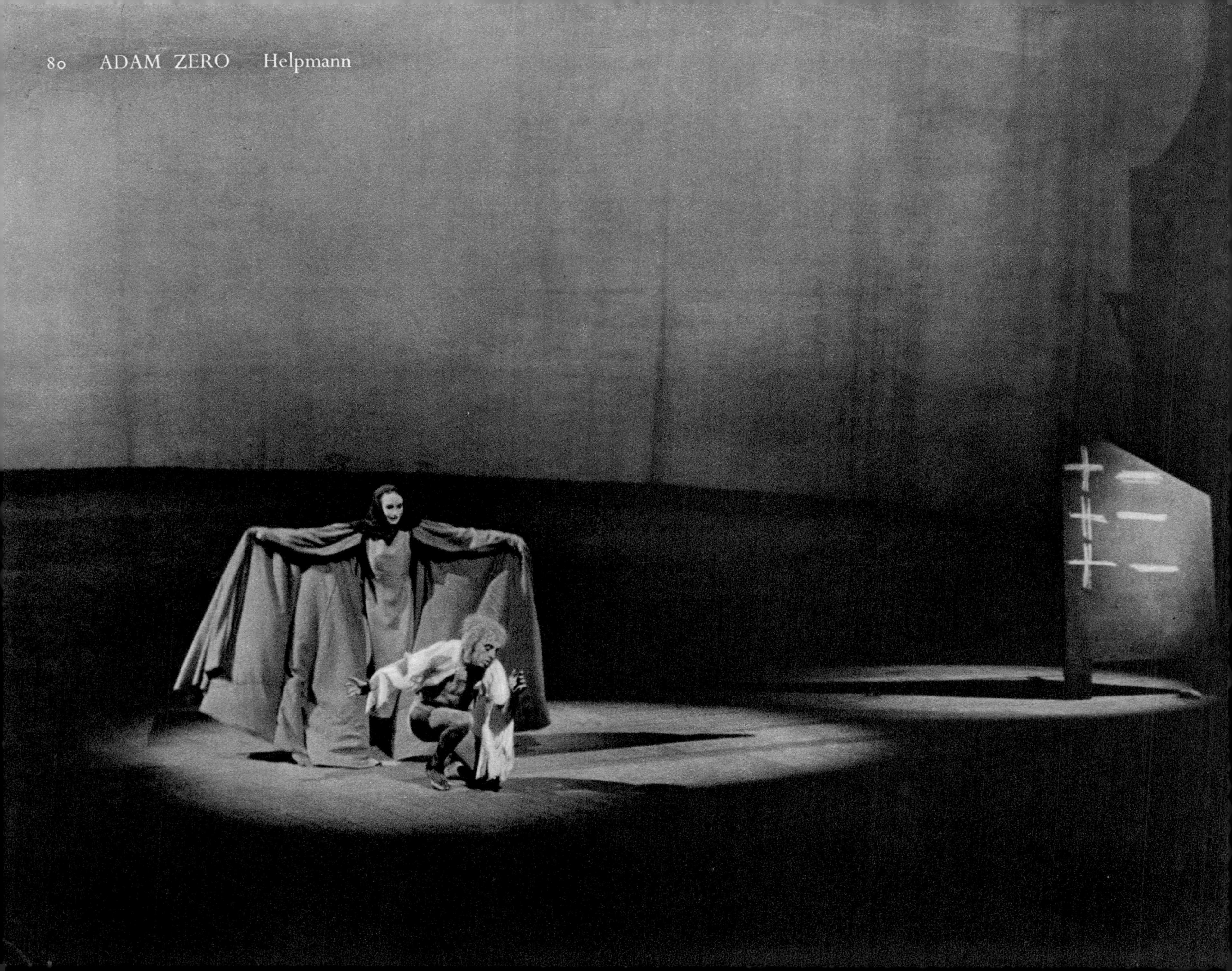

80 ADAM ZERO Helpmann